# THE NEW APHASIA WORKBOOK FOR ADULTS

*Speech Therapy Activities for Aphasia Rehabilitation*

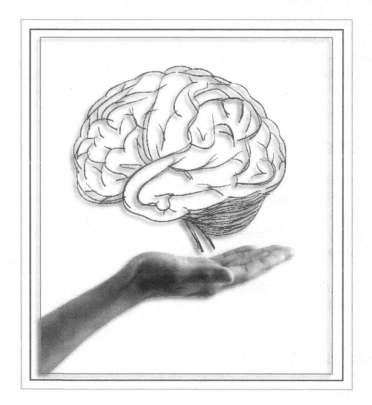

Author:

## Ruth J. Minner

# Table of content

## Section 1. Informative Handouts and Strategies

- What is Aphasia?
- Impacted Language Domains
- Caregiver Communication Tips
- Word Finding Strategies

## Section 2. Receptive Language

- Single-Stage Commands
- Two-Stage Commands
- Imitating Gestures with Objects
- Imitating Common Gestures
- Jigsaw puzzle
- Object Identification
- Healthy body activities
- Identifying road Signs
- Simple Yes/No Questions
- Guess who am I ?
- Understanding Gestures
- Alphabet ordinal numbers
- Numbers & Alphabet
- Which words fits?
- Sentence structure
- What's my job?
- Filling in Forms

## Section 3. Comprehension

- Auditory comprehension- mark to the object named.
- Reading Comprehension
- Letter recognition
- Word Matching with Pictures
- Word Matching without Pictures
- Sentence ID
- Functional Reading Comprehension
- Phrase completion
- Scripting

## Section 4. Expressive Language

- Picture Naming
- Expressing Object Functions
- Generative naming
- Completing Common Sentences
- Two-or-More-Word Responses
- Semantic Feature Analysis (SFA)
- Expanding Utterances

# Introduction

## What is Aphasia?

Aphasia is a communication disorder that affects a person's ability to understand or produce language.

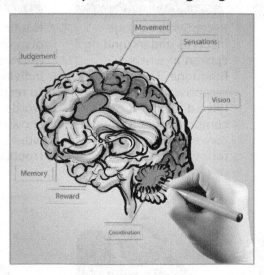

It is typically caused by damage to the brain, often resulting from a stroke, head injury, brain tumor, or neurological condition. Individuals with aphasia may have difficulty speaking, understanding speech, reading, and writing. The severity and symptoms of aphasia can vary widely, ranging from mild to severe impairment. Some people with aphasia may struggle to find the right words or form coherent sentences, while others may have trouble comprehending spoken or written language. Speech therapy and other interventions can help manage and improve aphasia symptoms.

## Symptoms of Aphasia

| | | |
|---|---|---|
| Trouble Speaking clearly | Trouble Remembering words | Trouble Remembering object names |
| Trouble Understanding speech | Trouble Writing clearly | Trouble Understanding written words |

# Impacted language domains of aphasia

**1**

## Expressive

This refers to the ability to produce language, including speaking and writing. Individuals with expressive aphasia may struggle to find words, form sentences, or write coherently.

**2**

## Receptive

Receptive language involves understanding spoken or written language. Those with receptive aphasia may have difficulty comprehending conversations, following instructions, or reading.

**3**

## Naming

Naming difficulty, also known as anomia, occurs when individuals struggle to recall or retrieve words. They may know the word they want to say but have trouble accessing it.

**4**

## Reading

Reading impairment, or alexia, can occur where individuals struggle to understand written words or sentences. This can range from difficulty recognizing letters to comprehending complex texts.

**5**

## Writing

Writing impairment, or agraphia, manifests as difficulty in producing written language. Individuals may have trouble forming letters, spelling words correctly, or organizing thoughts on paper.

**6**

## Auditory

This refers to the ability to understand spoken language. People with auditory comprehension difficulties may have trouble following conversations, understanding clues, or distinguishing between similar-sounding words.

**7**

## Verbal fluency

Verbal fluency refers to the ability to produce speech fluidly and quickly. Individuals with aphasia may experience reduced verbal fluency, resulting in pauses, hesitations, or difficulty expressing themselves smoothly.

These language domains may be affected to varying degrees in different types and severities of aphasia. Speech therapy and other interventions aim to address specific language deficits to improve communication skills and quality of life for individuals with aphasia.

# Caregiver communication tips in aphasia

Speak
Slowly
and
Clearly

Give
Them
Time to
Respond

Use
Visual
Aids

Confirm
Understanding

Use
Technology

Use
Simple
Language

Maintain
Eye
Contact
and Body
Language

Focus
on the
Message,
Not the
Mistakes

Encourage
Yes/No
Questions

Create
a
Supportive
Environment

# Word finding strategies in aphasia

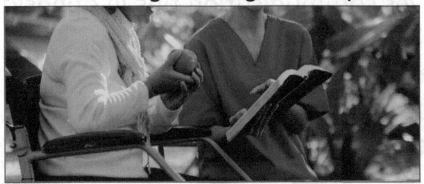

**Semantic Categorization:** Encourage the individual to group words by their meaning or category. For example, if they're trying to recall the word "apple", prompt them to think of other fruits or foods.

**Word Association:** Prompt the individual to think of words that are related to the target word. For example, if they're trying to remember "car" suggest words like "road", "drive" or "vehicle".

**Describe the Word:** Encourage the individual to describe the word they're trying to recall, including its attributes, function, or appearance. This can help trigger their memory. For example, if they're looking for "table" ,they might describe it as "a piece of furniture for eating or working".

**Phonemic Cues:** Provide phonemic cues by giving the individual the first sound or syllable of the target word. For example, if they're trying to recall "ball", say, "It starts with the sound 'buh'."

**Use Gestures:** Use gestures or pantomime to act out the meaning of the word. Sometimes, visual cues can help trigger word retrieval.

**Word Completion:** Provide the beginning of the word and ask the individual to complete it. For example, if they're trying to remember "elephant", say, "The word starts with 'eleph...'"

**Writing Practice:** Encourage the individual to write down the word they're trying to recall. Sometimes, the act of writing can help stimulate word retrieval.

**Chunking:** Break longer words or phrases into smaller, more manageable chunks. This can make it easier for the individual to recall the word. For example, if they're trying to remember "refrigerator", break it down into "re-frig-er-a-tor".

**Contextual Cues:** Provide contextual cues by giving clues or information about the situation in which the word is used. This can help trigger the individual's memory.

**Use of Alternative Words:** If the individual is unable to recall a specific word, encourage them to use alternative words or circumlocution to convey their meaning.

# Word finding strategies in aphasia

if you can't think of a word......

## Visualize it

Close your eyes and picture........

What the object looks like

## Draw it

Sketch a quick drawing........

How the object looks

## Describe it

Describe the object in the best way........

Explain its looks and category

## Associate it

Describe similar objects........

Think of other words that are associated or related to the object

## Gesture or point to it

Use your hands or fingers to act out the word ........

Point to the object if you can

## Try again

Rest and try again

This workbook offers a number of exercises aimed at enhancing various cognitive and linguistic skills.
This workbook serves as a guide for therapists to facilitate targeted interventions and for patients to engage in activities at their own pace.

# Word finding strategies in aphasia

<u>Example:-</u>      <u>Eating vegetable salad</u>

| Type | Example |
|---|---|
| **Category Cues:** | Provide a category or group of ingredients commonly found in salads. For example, you could say, "It's a dish made with vegetables like lettuce, tomatoes, and cucumbers." |
| **Functional Description:** | Describe the purpose or function of certain salad ingredients or utensils. For instance, you might say, "We use this tool to toss the salad and mix the ingredients evenly", while demonstrating the action of tossing with a salad fork or tongs. |
| **Contextual Cues:** | You could say, "We often enjoy this dish as a side during meals, especially in the summer." |
| **Visual Aids:** | Use pictures, illustrations, or actual salad ingredients to visually represent different components of a salad. This can help reinforce understanding and facilitate communication about salad ingredients and preparation methods. |
| **Word Completion:** | Provide the initial sound or syllable of the target word related to salad ingredients or actions. For example, if the individual is trying to remember the word "lettuce", you could say, "It starts with 'le...'" |
| **Opposite or Antonym:** | Provide the opposite of a salad-related concept to trigger recall. For instance, you could say, "This dish is typically served cold, unlike soup which is served hot." |
| **Associative Context:** | Provide a contextually relevant phrase or sentence associated with eating or preparing salad. For example, you could say, "We often dress our salads with vinaigrette or ranch dressing for added flavor." |

# Single-stage commands

Complete the statement.

## Morning Routine

Wake up early in the _____ .

Brush your _____ .

Take a _____ .

Get _____ .

Eat a healthy _____ .

# Single-stage commands

Do the activity yourself.

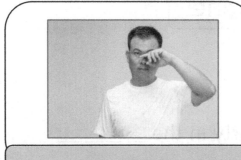

Touch your nose.

Wave your hand.

Blow a kiss.

Open your mouth.

Give a high five.

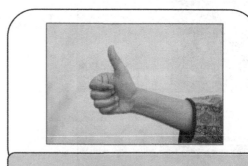

Thumbs up

Raise your arm.

Clap your hands.

# Two-stage commands

Match the numbers by tracing the line to the colors.
Find the colors of the numbers and color the circles.

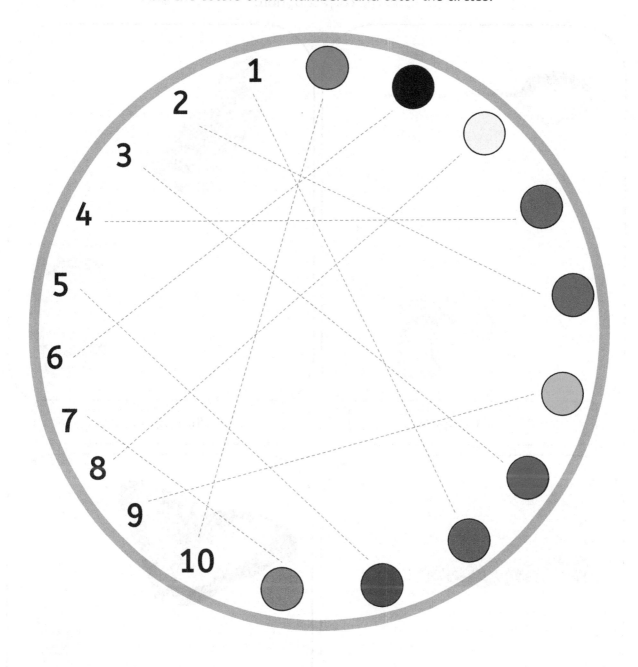

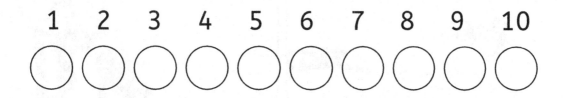

# Two-stage commands

Read the question.
Mark the correct option.

Which is a spoon?

Which is a glass?

Which is a toothbrush?

Which is a butterfly?

# Two-stage commands

Read the question.
Mark the correct option.

Which is  a cat?

Which is  a plant?

Which is  a bird?

Which is  a fruit?

# Imitating Gestures with Objects

What impression does the body language in each of these pictures give you?

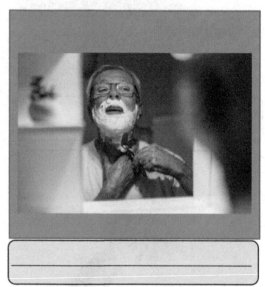

# Imitating Common Gestures

| Gesture | Date | Number of Repetitions |
|---|---|---|
| Waving | | |
| Thumbs Up | | |
| Pointing | | |
| Clapping | | |
| Shrugging | | |
| Nodding | | |
| Shaking Head  (No) | | |
| Blowing a Kiss | | |

**Reflection:** After completing your practice sessions, take a moment to reflect on your experiences:
Which gestures did you find easiest to imitate?
Were there any gestures that proved to be particularly challenging?
How do you feel about your progress in imitating gestures?
What strategies or techniques helped you improve your imitation skills?
**Notes:** Feel free to jot down any additional thoughts or observations during your practice. Remember, consistent practice and patience are key to improvement in aphasia therapy.

# Jigsaw Puzzle

Write the same numbers on all the pieces.

# Object Identification

Mark the correct option in each row.

## 1. Which one is a clock?

## 2. Which one is a pillow?

## 3. Which one is medicine?

 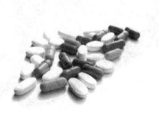

## 4. Which one is a newspaper?

# Object Identification

Mark the correct option in each row.

cup

comb

dolphin

dress

brush

butterfly

notebook

noodles

# Object Identification

Mark the correct option in each row.

## mug

## mirror

## camera

## cricket

## fruit salad

## fan

## lotus

## lamp

# Healthy Body Activities

Write how you would gesture to communicate the following...

I want _____

I want _____

# Healthy Body Activities

Write how you would gesture to communicate the following...

I want _____

I want _____

# Healthy Body Activities

Write how you would gesture to communicate the following...

I want _____

I want _____

# Identify Road Signs

Write the meaning of each sign on the line.

| Go ahead | Animal crossing | Turn left |
| --- | --- | --- |
| Turn left | Turn right | Pedestrian crossing |

_____

_____

_____

_____

_____

_____

# Yes/No Questions

Read the question.
Mark the correct option.

Is this a box?

yes ⬤   no ⬤

Is this a pen?

yes ⬤   no ⬤

Are these glasses?

yes ⬤   no ⬤

Are these nails?

yes ⬤   no ⬤

# Yes/No Questions

Read the question.
Mark the correct option.

1. Is the sun hot?                              Yes / no

2. Do you like ice cream?                       Yes / no

3. Is water wet?                                Yes / no

4. Do you wear shoes on your head?              Yes / no

5. Can birds swim?                              Yes / no

6. Is the sky blue?                             Yes / no

7. Do you sleep at night?                       Yes / no

8. Is a banana purple?                          Yes / no

9. Do you use a spoon to eat soup?              Yes / no

10. Is the moon made of cheese?                 Yes / no

11. Do you brush your teeth every day?          Yes / no

12. Is a cat a type of insect?                  Yes / no

# Yes/No Questions

Read the question.
Mark the correct option.

| | |
|---|---|
| 1.  Do you like to drink water? <br><br> Yes ☐ <br> No ☐ | 2. Is the grass blue? <br><br> Yes ☐ <br> No ☐ |
| 3. Do you use a fork to eat? <br><br> Yes ☐ <br> No ☐ | 4. Can you see the stars at night? <br><br> Yes ☐ <br> No ☐ |
| 5. Is a car used for reading? <br><br> Yes ☐ <br> No ☐ | 6. Do you need a key to unlock a door? <br><br> Yes ☐ <br> No ☐ |
| 7. Is a chair used for driving? <br><br> Yes ☐ <br> No ☐ | 8. Do you wear socks on your hands? <br><br> Yes ☐ <br> No ☐ |

# Yes/No Questions

Read the question.
Mark the correct option.

9. Can you hear birds chirping in the morning?

Yes ☐

No ☐

10. Is the Earth flat?

Yes ☐

No ☐

11. Do you need a pillow to sleep?

Yes ☐

No ☐

12. Is snow hot?

Yes ☐

No ☐

13. Can you see your reflection in a mirror?

Yes ☐

No ☐

14. Do you like to eat apples?

Yes ☐

No ☐

15. Is the sky usually blue during the day?

Yes ☐

No ☐

16. Is a book made of cookies?

Yes ☐

No ☐

# Guess Who I Am?

Write the correct animal name.

1. I am a big cat known for my distinctive black mane. I am native to Africa and a skilled hunter. Who am I?

- - - - - - - - - - - - - - - - - - - - - - - -

2. I am a marsupial found mainly in Australia. I carry my young in a pouch on my belly. Who am I?

- - - - - - - - - - - - - - - - - - - - - - - -

3. I am an intelligent marine mammal. I have a large forehead and am known for my playful behavior. Who am I?

- - - - - - - - - - - - - - - - - - - - - - - -

4. I am a large bird of prey known for my keen eyesight and powerful talons. I am often associated with wisdom. Who am I?

- - - - - - - - - - - - - - - - - - - - - - - -

# Guess Who I Am?

Write the correct answer.

I'm tall when I'm young and short when I'm old.
What am I?

- - - - - - - - - - - - - - - - - - - -

What has keys but can't open locks?

- - - - - - - - - - - - - - - - - - -

# Guess Who I Am?

Write the correct answer.

I have cities, but no houses. I have mountains, but no trees. I have water, but no fish. What am I?

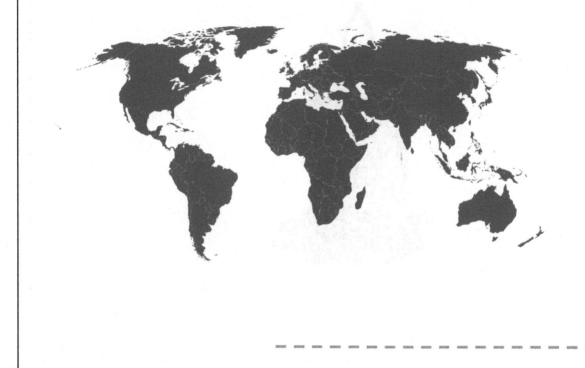

- - - - - - - - - - - - - - - - - - - - - - - -

What has a neck but no head?

- - - - - - - - - - - - - - - - - - - - - - - -

# Understanding Gestures

Match the hand gestures to the correct numbers.

# Understanding Gestures

Find and match the name with its hand gestures.

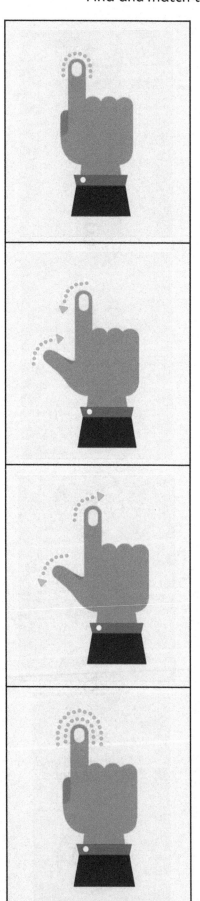

DOUBLE TAP

ZOOM IN

SINGLE TAP

ZOOM OUT

# Understanding Gestures

Find and match the name with its hand gestures.

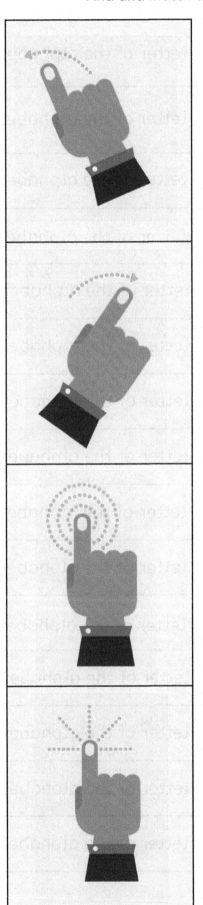

TOUCH & HOLD

FLICK RIGHT

TAP

FLICK LEFT

# Alphabet Ordinal Numbers

Complete the sentences using an ordinal word, for example: – first, second etc.

1. A is the _____ letter of the alphabet.

2. O is the _____ letter of the alphabet.

3. E is the _____ letter of the alphabet.

4. C is the _____ letter of the alphabet.

5. P is the _____ letter of the alphabet.

6. L is the _____ letter of the alphabet.

7. F is the _____ letter of the alphabet.

8. I is the _____ letter of the alphabet.

9. N is the _____ letter of the alphabet.

10. T is the _____ letter of the alphabet.

11. R is the _____ letter of the alphabet.

12. U is the _____ letter of the alphabet.

13. D is the _____ letter of the alphabet.

14. K is the _____ letter of the alphabet.

15. Z is the _____ letter of the alphabet.

# Which Words Fits?

## Mark the word.

Coffee

Water

Juice

Crayon

Chair

Table

Bed

Sofa

Car

Bicycle

Scooter

Airplane

Tooth brush

Comb

Clip

Scarf

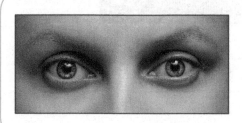

Eyes

Nose

Head

Ears

# Which Words Fits?

List items that fit each category or group below.

## Birthday party supplies

1. _____
2. _____
3. _____

## TV shows

1. _____
2. _____
3. _____

# Which Words Fits?

List items that fit each category or group below.

## songs

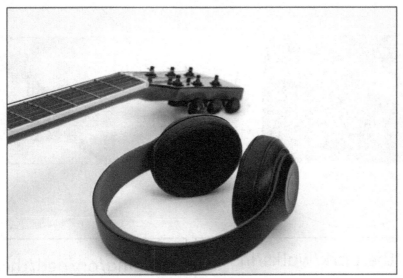

1. _____

2. _____

3. _____

## Things with wheels

1. _____

2. _____

3. _____

# Sentence Structure

Put the words in these sentences in the correct order.

The/dog/the/park/walks/in.

— — — — — — — — — — — — — —

jumping/on/bed/the/Children/were.

— — — — — — — — — — — — — —

ice-cream/delicious/ate/They.

— — — — — — — — — — — — — —

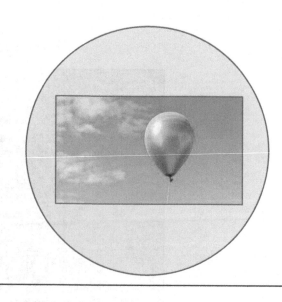

big/The/balloon/floated/high.

— — — — — — — — — — — — — —

# Sentence Structure

Put the words in these sentences in the correct order.

The/laughed/clown/the/kids/at.

_ _ _ _ _ _ _ _ _ _ _ _ _ _ _ _ _ _ _ _

on/the/sandcastle/beach/They/built/a.

_ _ _ _ _ _ _ _ _ _ _ _ _ _ _ _ _ _ _ _

on/the/rain/puddles/jumped/They.

_ _ _ _ _ _ _ _ _ _ _ _ _ _ _ _ _ _ _ _

hide-and-seek/played/They/happily.

_ _ _ _ _ _ _ _ _ _ _ _ _ _ _ _ _ _ _ _

# What's My Job?

Write the corresponding number on each picture.

1. I make furniture.

2. I treat sick people.

3. I teach in school.

4. I arrest criminals.

# What's My Job?

Write the corresponding number on each picture.

5. I sell newspapers.

6. I do tricks in a circus.

7. I cut hair.

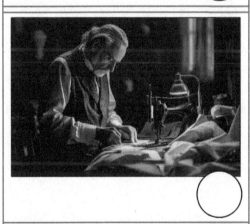

8. I make clothes.

# What's My Job?

Write the corresponding number on each picture.

9. I help people in court.

10. I grow vegetables.

11. I serve people in restaurant.

12. I build buildings and houses.

# Fill in the form

My name is Philip Jones.

I am 27 years old and come from Russia.

I am married and I have 2 kids.

I live with my family at 45 Pervomayskaya, Blvd 8/A, Apt 26, Vladimir.

Our postcode is TH1 2FG.

Our telephone number is 01235 889945.

I also have a mobile. My mobile number is 022663 874521.

I am learning WordPress.

Today I am joining the coaching classes.

| Pervomayskaya Coaching Classes | |
|---|---|
| Surname | |
| First name | |
| Address | |
| Postcode | |
| Age | |
| Occupation | |
| Mobile number | |
| Home tel | |

# Auditory Comprehension

Write the name of the object.

# Auditory Comprehension

Write the name of the object.

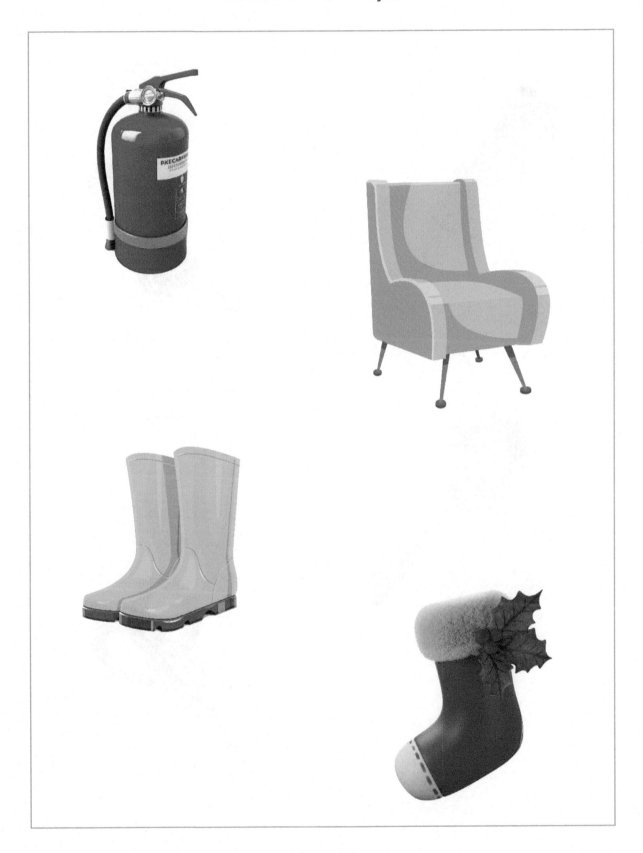

# Auditory Comprehension

Write the name of the object.

# Auditory Comprehension

Write the name of the object.

# Auditory Comprehension

Label the body parts.

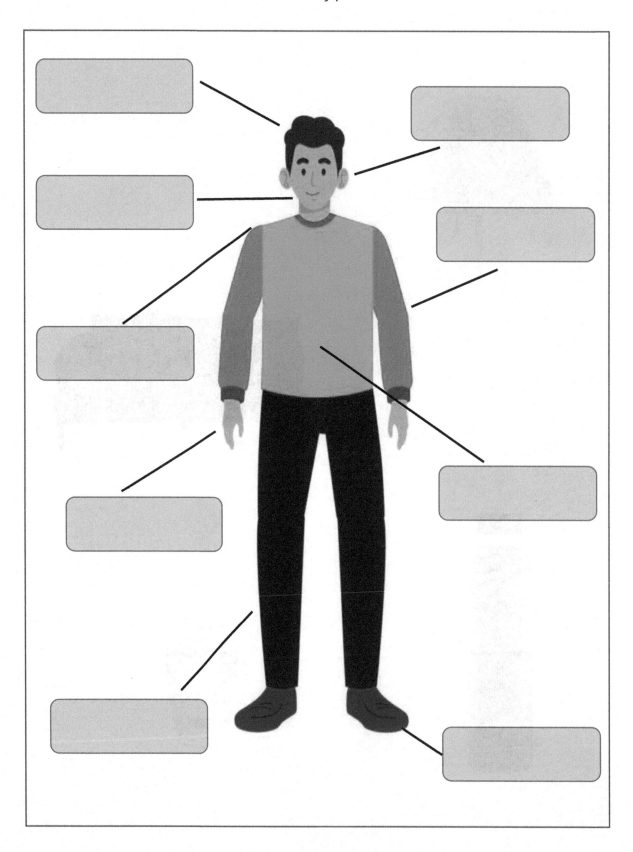

# Auditory Comprehension

Match the word to the associated picture.

Train

Owl

# Auditory Comprehension

Match the word to the associated picture.

Bicycle

Bus

# Auditory Comprehension

Match the word to the associated picture.

Dog

Turtle

# Auditory Comprehension

Match the word to the associated picture.

Shirt

Hat

# Reading Comprehension

Answer the following questions.

1. What time do you usually wake up in the morning?

a) Before 6:00 AM

b) Between 6:00 AM and 7:00 AM

c) After 7:00 AM

2. What is your morning beverage of choice?

a) Coffee

b) Tea

c) Juice

d) Other (please specify)

3. How do you typically start your day?

a) Exercise or stretching

b) Reading the newspaper

c) Checking emails or messages

d) Other (please specify)

4. What do you usually have for breakfast?

a) Cereal or oatmeal

b) Toast or bread with spreads

c) Eggs and bacon

d) Other (please specify)

5. How do you stay mentally active during the day?

a) Crossword puzzles or Sudoku

b) Reading books or magazines

c) Engaging in stimulating conversations

d) Other (please specify)

# Reading Comprehension

Answer the following questions.

6. What do you typically do for lunch?

a) Cook a meal at home

b) Eat out at a restaurant

c) Have a sandwich or salad

d) Other (please specify)

7. How do you like to spend your afternoons?

a) Running errands or shopping

b) Gardening or outdoor activities

c) Watching TV or listening to music

d) Other (please specify)

8. At what time do you usually have dinner?

a) Before 6:00 PM

b) Between 6:00 PM and 7:00 PM

c) After 7:00 PM

9. How do you unwind in the evenings?

a) Watching TV or movies

b) Engaging in hobbies or crafts

c) Relaxing with a book

d) Other (please specify)

10. Do you have any specific bedtime rituals?

a) Reading a book or listening to calming music

b) Meditating or practicing deep breathing exercises

c) Drinking a warm beverage like herbal tea

d) Other (please specify)

# Reading Comprehension

Answer the following questions.

11. How many meals do you typically have in a day?

a) Three (breakfast, lunch, dinner)

b) Four (including snacks)

c) Five or more

d) Other (please specify)

12. How often do you engage in physical activity?

a)   Daily

b) Few times a week

c) Rarely or never

13. What do you enjoy doing the most during your free time?

a) Spending time with family or friends

b) Pursuing hobbies or interests

c) Relaxing at home

d) Other (please specify)

14. Do you have any specific dietary restrictions or preferences?

a) Vegetarian or vegan

b) Gluten-free

c) No specific restrictions

15. How do you keep track of your daily schedule/appointments?

a) Using a physical planner or calendar

b) Using a smartphone or computer app

c) Memory and routine

# Reading Comprehension

Answer the following questions.

---

16. Do you take any medications or supplements regularly?

a) Yes

b) No

---

17. How do you maintain social connections?

a) Meeting friends in person

b) Phone calls or video chats

c) Social media

d) Other (please specify)

---

18. How do you manage stress or anxiety during the day?

a) Deep breathing exercises

b) Taking short breaks or walks

c) Practicing mindfulness or meditation

d) Other (please specify)

---

19. What role does spirituality or religion play in your daily routine?

a) Attending religious services or rituals

b) Engaging in personal prayers or meditation

c) None

---

20. What do you consider the most important aspect of your daily routine?

a) Staying physically active

b) Taking care of mental well-being

c) Other (please specify)

# Reading Comprehension

Memories of Spring

As the warmth of spring sun caresses the earth, memories of yesteryears bloom like flowers in the garden of my mind. I recall the laughter of children playing under the cherry blossom trees, their joyful shrieks echoing through the gentle breeze. The scent of freshly cut grass mingled with the perfume of blossoms, a fragrant symphony of nature's embrace. Each petal holds a story, each bloom a cherished moment, painting the canvas of nostalgia with hues of springtime magic.

Q.1- What memories does the warmth of spring evoke in the passage?

_____

_____

Q.2- Describe the scene of children playing under the cherry blossom trees.

_____

_____

Q.3- How does the passage describe the scent of spring?

_____

_____

Q.4- What does the author compare the memories to?

_____

_____

Q.5- How does the author depict the significance of each bloom in the passage?

_____

_____

# Reading Comprehension

Remembering Childhood Days

In the golden haze of reminiscence, childhood emerges like a cherished storybook. Days spent climbing trees, chasing butterflies, and building sandcastles by the shore flood the mind with warmth. Laughter echoed freely, carried by the winds of innocence, while imagination painted the world in vivid hues. Each memory, a treasure trove of simple joys, etched in the heart forevermore.

Q.1- What does the passage describe about childhood memories?

_____

_____

Q.2- Can you recall activities mentioned in the passage that you enjoyed during your childhood?

_____

_____

Q.3- How does the passage depict the role of laughter in childhood?

_____

_____

Q.4- What is the significance of imagination according to the passage?

_____

_____

Q.5- How would you describe the importance of childhood memories in shaping who we are?

_____

_____

# Letter Recognition

Match the uppercase letter to the lowercase letter.

| | | | |
|---|---|---|---|
| A | b | G | j |
| B | d | H | g |
| C | e | I | h |
| D | a | J | l |
| E | f | K | k |
| F | c | L | i |

| | | | |
|---|---|---|---|
| M | o | S | s |
| N | m | T | x |
| O | r | U | u |
| P | n | V | w |
| Q | q | W | v |
| R | p | X | t |

# Letter Recognition

Say and write the letter sound you hear at the beginning of the word.

 _ _ _ _ an  t

 _ _ _ _ issue  m

 _ _ _ _ lasses  f

 _ _ _ _ hair  g

_ _ _ _ irror c

# Letter Recognition

Say and write the letter sound you hear at the beginning of the word.

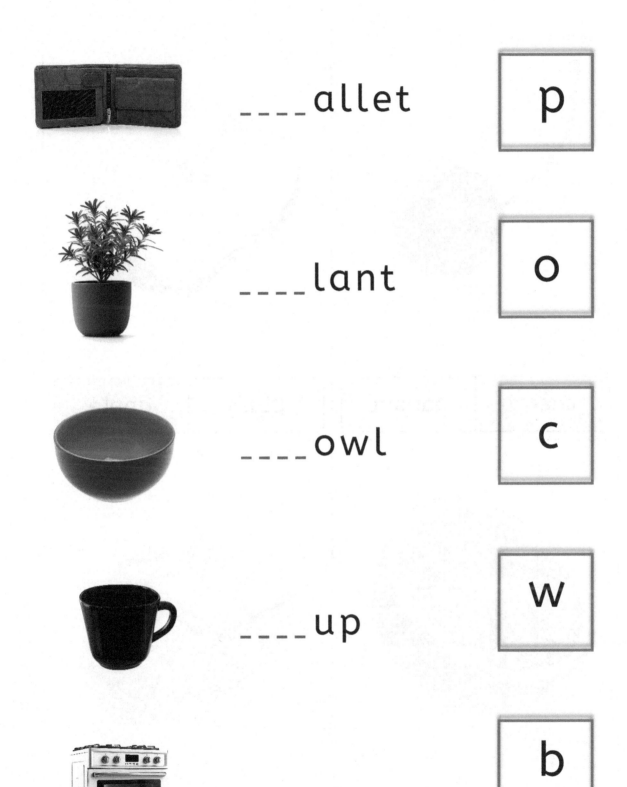

_ _ _ _ allet

p

_ _ _ _ lant

o

_ _ _ _ owl

c

_ _ _ _ up

w

_ _ _ _ ven

b

# Word Matching with Picture

Identify and match the picture with its name.

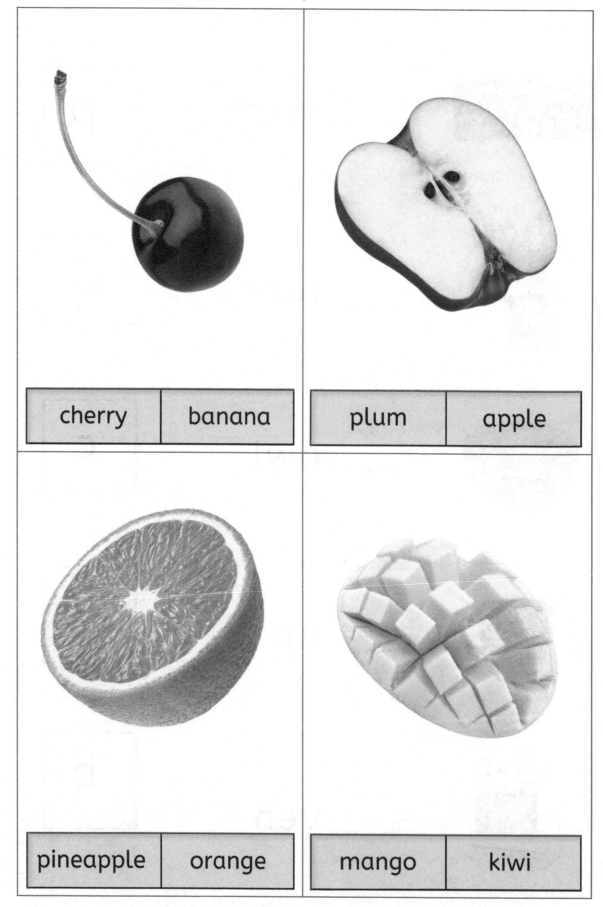

| cherry | banana |
|--------|--------|

| plum | apple |
|------|-------|

| pineapple | orange |
|-----------|--------|

| mango | kiwi |
|-------|------|

# Word Matching with Picture

Identify and match the picture with its name.

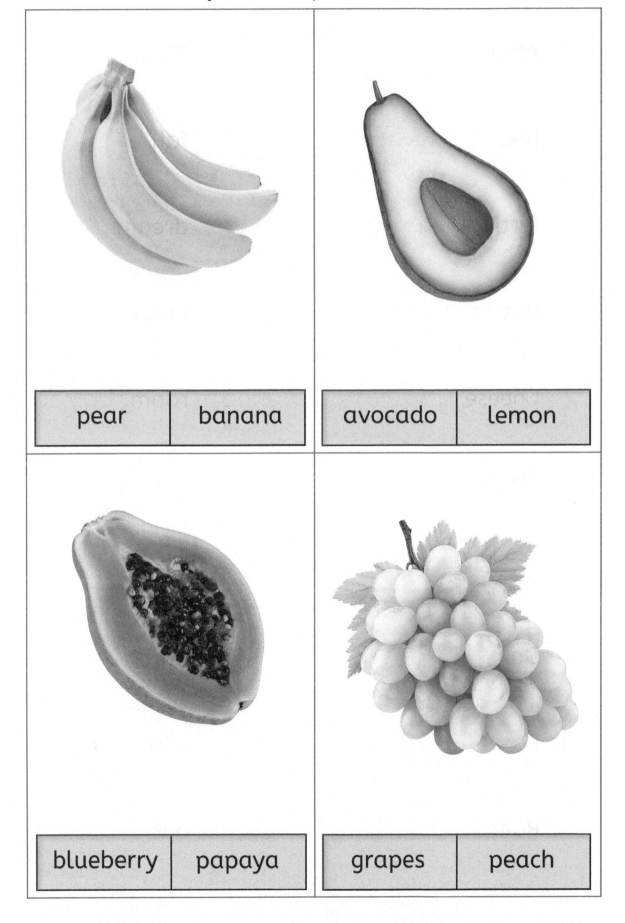

| pear | banana |
| avocado | lemon |

| blueberry | papaya |
| grapes | peach |

# Word Matching without Picture

Draw a line between words to make a compound word.

| After | flies |
|-------|-------|
| Bed | fall |
| Birth | dream |
| Butter | noon |
| Cheese | room |
| Clock | burger |
| Come | day |
| Day | port |
| Pass | wise |
| Rain | out |

# Sentence ID

Match the sentence to the correct picture.

I am watching TV.

I have a comb.

What is the time?

# Sentence ID

Match the sentence to the correct picture.

I want to sleep.

I want to look in a
mirror.

I need my medicine.

# Functional Reading Comprehension

Circle the items on today's menu.

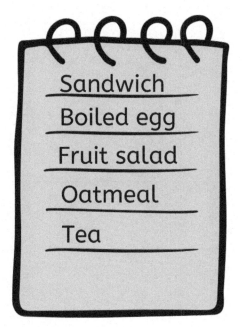

# Phrase Completion

Complete the phrase.

Good _____

How are _____

Thank _____

Come _____

Go over_____

Yes or_____

Hot or _____

Left or _____

Wash my _____

Brush my _____

Comb my _____

Close the _____

Heavy or _____

# Phrase Completion

Complete the phrase.

I take my coffee with _____

I am tired and I'd like to go to _____

I drink my tea from a _____

I want to read a _____

I have a sister and a _____

I have a mom and a _____

I want to sit in my _____

I have a son and a _____

Cut the ribbon with a pair of _____

Before I leave the house, I look in the _____

I wash my _____

To shave, I need to use a _____

I drive a _____

# Phrase Completion

Complete the phrase.

"I remember when I first learned to ride..."

_____

"Back in my day, we would often gather around the table for..."

_____

"During my younger years, I loved to spend time playing..."

_____

"When I was a child, I often helped my parents with..."

_____

"As an older person, I still enjoy the taste of..."

_____

"In the past, I frequently listened to music on..."

_____

"During my prime, I would always make time for..."

_____

"I have fond memories of playing with toys such as..."

_____

# Phrase Completion

Complete the phrase.

"Growing up, I often spent evenings reading books like..."

"Looking back, I recall the excitement of..."

"During my formative years, I would often visit..."

"In my generation, it was typical to show respect by..."

"As an elder, I've learned to appreciate the value of..."

"Recalling my younger days, I often dreamed of..."

"Nostalgically, I reminisce about the sound of..."

"Through the years, I've experienced the joys and challenges of..."

# Scripting

Write your response.

I live in _____

I sleep in _____

# Scripting

Write your response.

I take showers in _____

I prepare meals in _____

# Scripting

Write your response.

I eat my meal in _____

I enjoy evening tea in _____

# Picture Naming

Name the object and explain its usages.

Name:-
_Toothbrush_

Usages:-
_Used for cleaning teeth every morning and night._

Name:-
_____

Usages:-
_____

# Picture Naming

Name the object and explain its usages.

Name:- _____

Usages:- _____

---

Name:- _____

Usages:- _____

# Picture Naming

Name the object and explain its usages.

Name:-
_____

Usages:-
_____

Name:-
_____

Usages:-
_____

# Expressing Object Functions

Match the picture with its correct option.

Take a picture

Lock a door

Keep my hands warm

To drink

To eat

Keep my feet warm

Clean my body

# Expressing Object Functions

Write the name of the object.

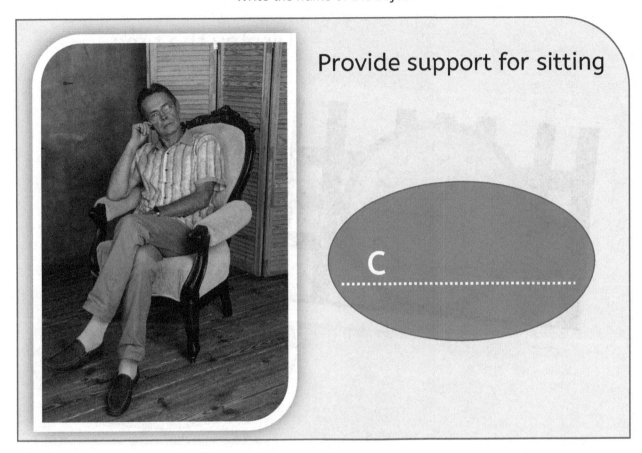

## Provide support for sitting

C _____

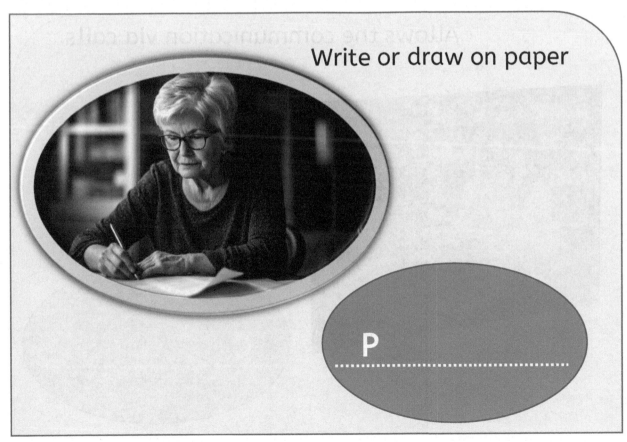

## Write or draw on paper

P _____

# Expressing Object Functions

Write the name of the object.

## Display the time

M ..............................................

## Allows the communication via calls

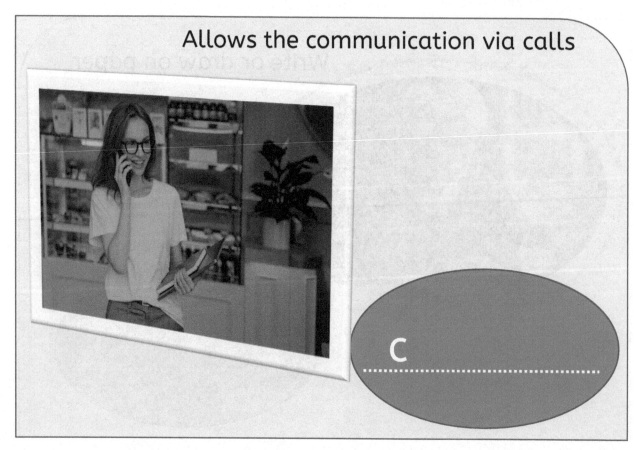

C ..............................................

# Expressing Object Functions

Write the name of the object.

## Absorbs moisture from the body

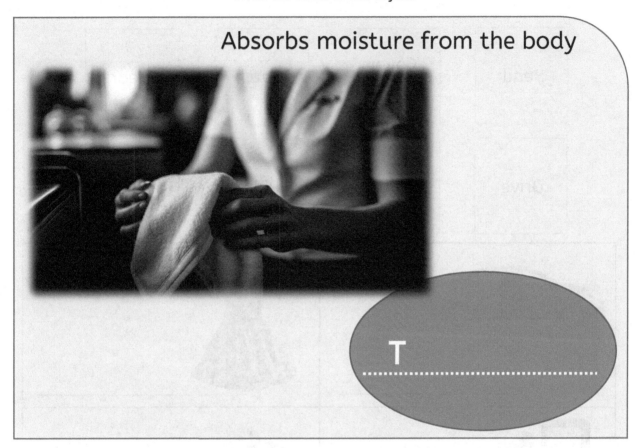

T ..............................................

## Contains written information for reading

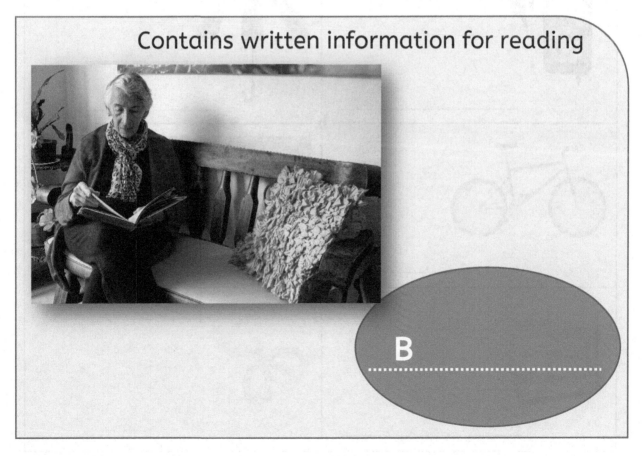

B ..............................................

# Expressing Object Functions

Write the functions.

| | | | |
|---|---|---|---|
| Read | Cover rain | Watch | Wear |
| Drive | Cut | Ride | Listen |

| | |
|---|---|
| _____ | _____ |
| _____ | _____ |
| _____ | _____ |
| _____ | _____ |

# Generative Naming

Write 10 things you see in the pictures.

**HOME**

| | |
|---|---|
| 1. | 6. |
| 2. | 7. |
| 3. | 8. |
| 4. | 9. |
| 5. | 10. |

# Generative Naming

Write 10 things you see in the pictures.

**PARK**

| | |
|---|---|
| 1. | 6. |
| 2. | 7. |
| 3. | 8. |
| 4. | 9. |
| 5. | 10. |

# Generative Naming

Write 10 things you see in the pictures.

**BEDROOM**

| | |
|---|---|
| 1. | 6. |
| 2. | 7. |
| 3. | 8. |
| 4. | 9. |
| 5. | 10. |

# Generative Naming

Write 10 things you see in the pictures.

## LIVING ROOM

| | |
|---|---|
| 1. | 6. |
| 2. | 7. |
| 3. | 8. |
| 4. | 9. |
| 5. | 10. |

# Generative Naming

Write 10 things you see in the pictures.

**KITCHEN**

| 1. | 6. |
|---|---|
| 2. | 7. |
| 3. | 8. |
| 4. | 9. |
| 5. | 10. |

# Generative Naming

Write 10 things you see in the pictures.

**BANK**

| | |
|---|---|
| 1. | 6. |
| 2. | 7. |
| 3. | 8. |
| 4. | 9. |
| 5. | 10. |

# Generative Naming

Write 10 things you see in the pictures.

## CLASS ROOM

| 1. | 6. |
|---|---|
| 2. | 7. |
| 3. | 8. |
| 4. | 9. |
| 5. | 10. |

# Complete Common Sentences

Use the correct word card from the word bank to complete the common sentence.

| | | | | |
|---|---|---|---|---|
| trees | sunsets | color | garden | sky |
| sound | beautiful | crickets | outside | skin |

1. "The flowers in the garden are so _____."

2. "Look at the birds flying in the _____."

3. "The _____ provide shade on hot days."

4. "I love listening to the _____ of rain."

5. "The _____ here are breathtaking."

6. "The breeze feels nice on my _____."

7. "I enjoy watching butterflies in the _____."

8. "The leaves are changing _____ in the autumn."

9. "The sound of _____ chirping is soothing."

10. "Let's sit _____ and enjoy the fresh air."

# Two-or-more-word Responses

Write the complete name.

| Wheel+chair | Medi+cine | News+paper |
| Note+book | Hair+brush | Air+plane |
| Pony+tail | Milk+shake | Sand+wich |

# Semantic Feature Analysis (SFA)

Fill in the boxes with the correct answers.

| Group/category | Use | Location |
|---|---|---|
| This is…… | This is used to/for…… | This is found…… |

| Properties | Association | Function |
|---|---|---|
| This feel, looks, taste like…… | Is reminds me of…… | This gives…… |

| Group/category | Use | Location |
|---|---|---|
| This is…… | This is used to/for…… | This is found…… |

| Properties | Association | Function |
|---|---|---|
| This feel, looks, taste like…… | Is reminds me of…… | This gives…… |

# Semantic Feature Analysis (SFA)

Fill in the boxes with the correct answers.

| Group/category<br>This is…… | Use<br>This is used to/for…… | Location<br>This is found…… |
|---|---|---|
| **Properties**<br>This feel, looks, taste like…… | **Association**<br>Is reminds me of…… | **Function**<br>This gives…… |

| Group/category<br>This is…… | Use<br>This is used to/for…… | Location<br>This is found…… |
|---|---|---|
| **Properties**<br>This feel, looks, taste like…… | **Association**<br>Is reminds me of…… | **Function**<br>This gives…… |

# Semantic Feature Analysis (SFA)

Fill in the boxes with the correct answers.

| Group/category | Use | Location |
|---|---|---|
| This is…… | This is used to/for…… | This is found…… |

| Properties | Association | Function |
|---|---|---|
| This feel, looks, taste like…… | Is reminds me of…… | This gives…… |

| Group/category | Use | Location |
|---|---|---|
| This is…… | This is used to/for…… | This is found…… |

| Properties | Association | Function |
|---|---|---|
| This feel, looks, taste like…… | Is reminds me of…… | This gives…… |

# Expanding Utterances

Match the words in each list to create a sentence about the photograph.

| doctor | | students |
|--------|--------|----------|
| singer | treats | patients |
| chef | | pipes |

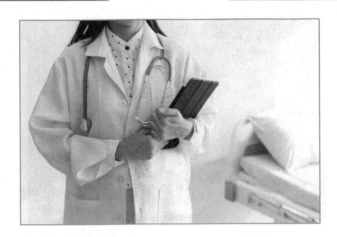

A _____ treats _____

---

| author | | food |
|--------|--------|------|
| singer | writes | home |
| architect | | book |

An _____ writes _____

# Expanding Utterances

Match the words in each list to create a sentence about the photograph.

| singer | | food |
|--------|--|------|
| chef | prepared | poem |
| sweeper | | song |

A _____ prepared _____

---

| poet | | hair |
|------|--|------|
| dentist | fixes | eyes |
| singer | | teeth |

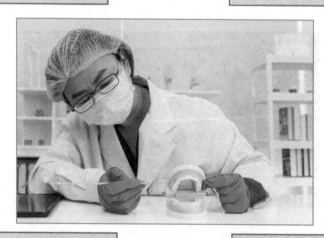

A _____ fixes _____

# Expanding Utterances

Match the words in each list to create a sentence about the photograph.

| teacher | | plates |
|---------|---|--------|
| lawyer | teaches | chair |
| engineer | | students |

A [ _____ ] teaches [ _____ ]

---

| baker | | cakes |
|-------|---|-------|
| painter | bakes | fan |
| cashier | | building |

A [ _____ ] bakes [ _____ ]

# Expanding Utterances

Match the words in each list to create a sentence about the photograph.

| artist | | eggs |
| soldier | grows | vegetables |
| farmer | | books |

A [        ] grows [        ]

---

| waiter | | train |
| journalist | drives a | bus |
| bus driver | | school |

A [        ] drives a [        ]

# Expanding Utterances

Provide a thorough description of the image, including all the details you can observe.

Describe

Describe

# Expanding Utterances

Provide a thorough description of the image, including all the details you can observe.

## Describe

---

## Describe

# Expanding Utterances

Provide a thorough description of the image, including all the details you can observe.

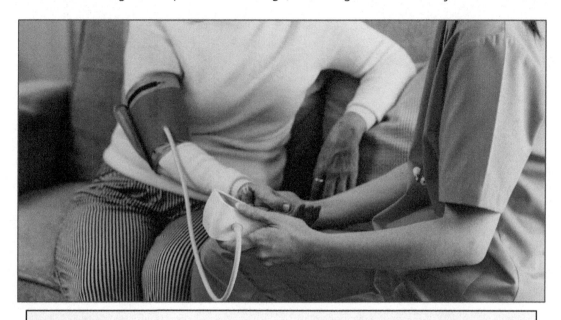

## Describe

## Describe

Made in United States
North Haven, CT
05 December 2024

61743290R00057